Spilling the Beans on...

Buffalo Bill

and other wild west show-offs

by Dennis Hamley

Illustrations   Mike Mosedale

PUBLISHING

About the author

Dennis Hamley lives in Hertford with his wife and two cats. He has a son who is a scientist, a daughter in publishing and a grandson.

He has written many children's books. *The War and Freddy* was shortlisted for the Smarties Prize. He writes mysteries for a children's crime series, including *Death Penalty* and *Deadly Music*, and is now writing six mysteries set in the Middle Ages. He also writes football, ghost, animal and railway stories.

He often visits schools for talks and he also runs creative writing courses.

Contents

CHAPTER 1

"Winner Take All"

Well, here we are at one of the big fights of the 19th century. We've got a ringside seat, so let's sit back and enjoy it.

I can't wait.
You don't have to. Here's the MC. He's shouting his head off.

"Ladies and Gentlemen. Here is a contest to the death for the Wild West championship of America, between, in the red corner, weighing in at one mighty ton, the reigning champion: THE BUFFALO. In the blue corner, weighing in at 12 stone: BILL CODY.

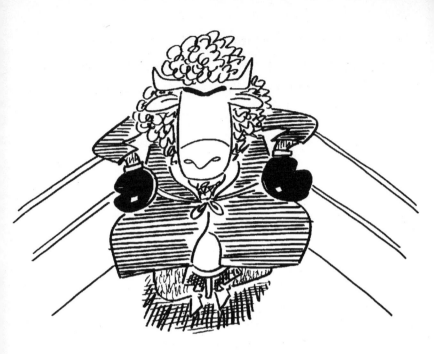

Let's have a clean, fair fight and may the best man – or animal – win and may the WINNER TAKE ALL. Seconds out, round one."

Well, be sure of this. The fight wasn't very clean and it certainly wasn't fair. As animals go, the buffalo, I hate to tell you, is a bit stupid, very slow and can't shoot rifles. William Frederick Cody was far from stupid and was a brilliant shot. And buffaloes had to be got rid of.

Why bother getting rid of them if they were stupid?
Because the great native American tribes – Sioux, Cheyenne,

Pawnee, Apache – hunted them for food, with bows and arrows, not rifles. Get rid of the buffaloes and what would the Indians eat? Get rid of the Sioux, Cheyenne, Pawnee and Apache and the Wild West could be opened up to the Europeans wanting land in their new country.

And then what?
If there were no buffaloes roaming the plains then ranchers would have room for their new herds of cattle. The world would be ready for McDonalds.

Just think, if William Cody hadn't turned up with his gun (and many others with him, of course; he made sure he was the one everybody knew about), instead of beefburgers we might be eating buffburgers.

But William F. Cody shot so many buffaloes that he became famous for it. So that's what he was always called:

BUFFALO BILL.

Winner take all? He even took their name.

He was a crack shot and a marvellous scout who could follow trails nobody else could. Stories about his incredible deeds spread across America. He was the scourge of the Indians and then their great friend and protector. He appeared in plays (always playing himself) and then ran his own Wild West show, which wowed America, then Europe, then everywhere else.

Yes, truly one of the Wild West's great heroes. No wonder everybody said he was wonderful.

But stick around and you may hear different. There was a lot more to Buffalo Bill than meets the eye. And there were a lot of people in his story.

So, if Buffalo Bill was a great showman, then first of all we must meet the supporting cast.

Just a minute. Before that, why did you start talking about 'native Americans' and then change it to 'Indians'?
A good question. The Sioux, Cheyenne, Apache and the rest are the real native Americans. They were there countless centuries before the people we call 'American' turned up from Europe. Never forget that the 'Indian Wars' which made Buffalo Bill famous were nothing but a lot of new people with guns taking

what wasn't theirs away from an ancient people with bows and arrows. Nobody should feel proud of it.

The first Europeans called native Americans 'Indians' simply because they didn't know where they were. They thought that India would be the first land they reached when they sailed west. The name, with the addition of 'Red', stuck. The only reason I use it in this book is because that's what Buffalo Bill and everybody else called them. To go on saying 'native American' every time would sound weird. But that doesn't mean I don't think it's right.

★　　★　　★　　★

CHAPTER 2

Who's Who in the Story of Buffalo Bill

Isaac and Mary Cody, parents
Farmers in Iowa. But farming wasn't enough for Isaac. He followed the gold rush west in 1849, and took Mary and their children with him. Much good did it do him, because he didn't get very far.

Mary was English, Isaac was Irish. Buffalo Bill claimed he was descended from the ancient High Kings of Ireland. Well, who isn't?

Louisa Frederici

Buffalo Bill's wife. Poor woman. Or was she? She had a mind of her own. She kept throwing him out. He always came back. So she tried to keep him at home. No good. He would go away again, for months or years at a time. She was often starving while he was at home – he drank all the money. She was rich when he was away – he sent fortunes back. So which was better for Louisa – Buffalo Bill at home or as far away as possible?

Here's a clue. At Buffalo Bill's funeral, Louisa stood by the coffin. Six more women stood on the other side. Louisa looked at them and said, "Are they Bill's old girlfriends? I wouldn't put it past him." The other women said, "You'll never know, will you?"

Ned Buntline

Real name Edward Zane Carroll Judson. As Ned Buntline, he wrote novels costing a dime (something like 10p today) about the Wild West. Mostly they told of his own adventures. This included the time he was hanged (the rope broke). When he ran out of ideas, he went west to find more and there he met Buffalo Bill.

Ned claimed he discovered Buffalo Bill and made him famous. Ah, but did he? We shall see.

Grand Duke Alexis of Russia

Who? You don't believe me, do you? Well, it's true. Buffalo Bill took him on buffalo hunts across the great American Plains – and many other royals as well. They loved it. So did he.

Gordon Bennett

He owned the New York Herald, a big newspaper. He was into everything. He sent the reporter Henry Stanley to Africa to look for the lost explorer Dr Livingstone. It was Bennett who first took Buffalo Bill east to meet high society in Chicago and New York.

General Sheridan

In charge of the US Army fighting the Indians.Sheridan made Bill chief scout to the 5th cavalry and gave him the same pay as a colonel.

But did that make Bill Colonel William F. Cody, as he claimed?

Chief Tall Bull

Tall Bull. Sioux chief and terror of the US army. Killing Tall Bull was one of Buffalo Bill's greatest deeds. So they said. In fact it was Major Frank North who killed him.

Chief Yellow Hand

Cheyenne Chief. He fought Buffalo Bill in single combat. "I know you, Pahaska," Yellow Hand shouted. "Come out and fight with me."
'Pahaska' meant 'Long Yellow Hair'. This was odd, because Buffalo Bill's hair was brown. Perhaps Yellow Hand was calling out someone else after all. Anyway, they fought and Bill won – or so the story goes. Then he scalped the great chief.

Afterwards, 'Pahaska' was one of Bill's many nicknames and Yellow Hand's scalp was his greatest possession.

By the way, Bill really did win the duel. Though some say Yellow Hand only had a tomahawk, while Bill had a Winchester rifle. How could they possibly think such a thing?

Chief Sitting Bull

The greatest chief of all. A Sioux, but he united all the tribes against the US army. Beat – no, destroyed – General Custer at the Battle of the Little Big Horn (General Custer? A bit of a twerp, really. At least, General Sheridan thought so). Much later, Sitting Bull gave up fighting and even joined Buffalo Bill's Wild West show where he became a great friend of –

Little Annie Oakley

What a lady! Not five feet tall, yet the greatest shot in the west. If it hadn't been for her, Buffalo Bill's Wild West show might have folded years before. But everybody flocked to see her and her incredible feats with a rifle.

16

Wild Bill Hickok

Not to be confused with Buffalo Bill, though people always have. The other great hero of the Wild West. They were friends and rivals, and each was as big a rogue as the other. Some people thought Buffalo Bill did some of the things Wild Bill did and Buffalo Bill never said they were wrong – at least, not until after Wild Bill Hickok was dead.

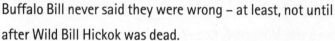

(PS. Sorry about that. It's just that there were a lot of Bills in the Wild West.)

Major John Burke, or 'Arizona John'

He was neither a major nor had he ever been anywhere near Arizona. He was a newspaperman and brilliant at public relations. As soon as he turned up, Buffalo Bill didn't want to know poor Ned Buntline any more. Arizona John Burke made the Wild West show the most successful entertainment the world had ever seen. Buffalo Bill would have been finished without him.

And without someone else as well. He was:

17

Nate Salsbury

An orphan who ran away to join the army at 15. He was
sentenced to death, released, and started managing theatres.
He saw how big Wild West shows could be, joined Buffalo Bill
and made sure that, once John Burke had got the audiences in,
they had something really amazing to watch.

Any more?

Plenty. But that's enough to be going on with.

So, who was William F. Cody?

Was he – the noble descendant of ancient kings?

Was he – Buffalo Bill, the fast-shooting, brave hero of the
Wild West?

Was he – Colonel William F. Cody, loyal and dependable officer
of the United States Army and the finest scout of them all?

Was he – Pahaska, scourge of the Indian tribes, who then
became their friend and champion?

Was he – Buffalo Bill, the great showman, friend of kings and
princes, who brought the Wild West to the rest of the world?

Was he all of these things?

Or none?

Wait and see.

CHAPTER 3

The Boyhood of Buffalo Bill

Just now you said Bill's father Isaac went looking for gold but "Much good did it do him." What does that mean?
Bill was only three when they went west in 1849. They didn't get very far. They settled in Kansas, a state in the midwest of America. Isaac built a log cabin on the Salt Lake Trail, where the wagon trains passed, and started trading with them. He thought he could make a fortune.

Did he?
He would have done. BUT:

Already, things were boiling up for the American Civil War which would happen twelve years later. The southern states believed in keeping black people as slaves. The northern states didn't. The southern states said they would secede (leave) the United States because of it. That meant they would leave the Union and go it alone. The war was fought to keep them in the United States, whether they liked it or not.

When Bill was a boy, the arguments were just starting. Isaac was against slavery.

Good for him. Why should that stop him making a fortune?
Because everybody else in Kansas thought different.

He could still make his fortune, couldn't he?
All right, what would you do? Remember:

 Everyone disagrees with you.

 They carry guns and knives and aren't slow in using
them, whether on Indians or each other.

 Even apart from that, life is hard round here anyway.

Would you:

a) say, "Perhaps this isn't the right place for me after all" and
go somewhere where people thought the same as you?

b) shut up about it and hope nobody found out?

c) shout your mouth off as loud as you could to all and sundry?

Well, whatever I'd do and whatever you'd do, Isaac did c).
Guess what happened.

I shudder to think.
You're right. One day in 1855, Isaac was riding home with little

eight-year-old Bill when he saw a big crowd of people, mostly drunk and all angry. He also saw a wooden box, which he thought was a platform for speakers. So he got off his horse, got on the box and started making an anti-slavery speech.

Did they listen?
They did not. They shouted at him and then rushed the soapbox. He was stabbed very nastily. But he didn't die. Bill rescued him. A few men helped get Isaac on to a wagon and they took him home.

I bet that shut him up.
Don't you believe it. Isaac was so angry that as soon as he was better, he went off to join an army pledged to fight the slavers.

And left Bill and his mother behind?

That's right. The neighbours made life rotten for them. It was no better when Isaac came home two years later to die. So now Bill was the breadwinner for the family. He was only 11.

Well, he was fed up with school. Anyway, he had to leave. He'd built a playhouse for little Mary Hyatt and stabbed another boy, Steve Gobel, in the leg for knocking it down. Bill said he was "dead in love" with little Mary. But Steve's father and the constable were after him now, so he went off with a wagon train for 40 days to keep out of their way.

Are these stories true?

Buffalo Bill said so. Who can tell? He also stopped a stampede of buffaloes by himself and killed his first Indian – all when he

was 11. Even if they aren't true, you can see why Buffalo Bill started being a hero very early in life.

Oh, come on, is there anything said about him that's true?
Yes. His first job. A big freight firm took him on to herd the cattle which followed the wagon trains. $40 a month. Not bad.

But he was only 11.
I know. But the boss of the firm, Alexander Majors, said, "We'll pay him a man's wages because he can ride a pony just as well as any man can."

It was on this trip that he killed his first Indian. So they say.

I bet his mother was proud of him.
No, she wasn't. She was furious. She made him come home and return to school. But he ran off the moment he could, back on the wagon trains.

Then what?
She got him back. So he went again. She got him back again. Off he went again. It couldn't last.

Why not?
When he was 12, Bill could:

a) ride and shoot better than most grown men and hold down jobs they couldn't do.

b) communicate in sign language to Indians as easily as speaking out loud.

c) speak the language of the Sioux as well as if he were one of them himself.

BUT Bill could not:

a) read.

b) write his own name.

So he thought he'd better try school one last time. After three months of education, he'd sorted it. And he was brilliant at using numbers. Later in life, he needed to be.

What then?
Well, no-one could stop him now. He went:

 Gold prospecting (he didn't find any).

 Fur trapping (Wild West pioneers wore furs just as much as rich women in the East).

Riding for the Pony Express, the fastest postal delivery till the railroads came. Pony Express riders, riding in relays of 45 miles each, could take letters 2,000

miles in eight days. But it was dangerous. Bill had to keep dodging hostile Indians.

Anything else?
Yes. The great wars with the Indians hadn't really started yet. Even so, there were often clashes. Bill went on a skirmish in 1860. Nobody knows how many Indians were killed, if any, but Bill boasted that they rounded up 100 horses and drove them back home.

It doesn't matter. What matters is that the party was led by:

WILD BILL HICKOK.

A fateful meeting.

What matters even more is that next year, 1861, the American Civil War started.

CHAPTER 4

Buffalo Bill the Great Hero

I bet Bill joined up straight away, didn't he?
Far from it. The Civil War started in 1861 but Bill stayed out.

Why? I thought he would have loved it.
Because his mother made him promise not to fight. She was tired of worrying about him.

So he never did?
Oh yes. In 1863, his mother died. But he still didn't join up. He was a scout for soldiers guarding against Indians and he earned $150 a month. Who would give up that sort of money? Not Bill.

Until...

One night he got into a wild party and when he woke up –
HE'D JOINED THE ARMY FIGHTING FOR THE NORTH
AGAINST THE SOUTH. He didn't remember a thing about it!

He must have been a great war hero.
Sadly, no. He never even claimed to be, though others did a lot
of claiming for him.

So what did he do in the war?
He got married.

Is that all?
Judging by what happened afterwards, it was quite enough.

For now he met:

LOUISA FREDERICI

Union with her was not a marriage made in Heaven.

How did they meet?
Ned Buntline said Bill rescued her from a mob of drunken soldiers. He snatched her up and whisked her away on his horse. Louisa said that her cousin brought him to their house in St Louis. Bill pulled her chair from under her, she scrambled up and slapped his face. Bill said nothing.

How did they get on?
Badly. The war ended in 1865. Bill bought a hotel, they got married the next year and the hotel went bankrupt. This was because Bill kept giving free drinks to all his friends. There was

only one other way to make quick money – to work on the railroad, which was steadily spreading westwards.

But as soon as he got there, who should he see but his old mate *Wild Bill Hickok*. Fatal. Neither of them ever got as far as the railroad.

So what did they do?
Well, now I come to think of it, this wasn't fatal at all. If Bill had ended up spiking track on to sleepers, nobody would have heard of him again. But Wild Bill Hickok made a suggestion that was one of the most important things anyone ever said to Buffalo Bill.

Was it:

a) "Stop messing around, Bill, and go home to your wife"?

b) "Let's rob a bank"?

c) "Let's go to the nearest bar and get drunk"?

It wasn't a). Wild Bill would never say such a thing. He wasn't called 'Wild' for nothing. Even if he did, Buffalo Bill wouldn't do it. He'd be too scared of Louisa.

It wasn't b), luckily for both of them. Though it could easily have been.

Wild Bill said c). Well, he would, wouldn't he?

But after a few drinks in the bar, Wild Bill Hickok said they should go off and be scouts for the army on the far western frontier following trails and guiding them through the rough country. So off they went. And now Buffalo Bill met:

GENERAL SHERIDAN

General Sheridan was looking for scouts he could trust. The requirements were:

a) knowing the land.

b) knowing all about Indians.

c) having, General Sheridan said, "endurance and courage."

Whatever Buffalo Bill's faults, nobody could say he didn't measure up to these better than anyone – except Wild Bill Hickok. So General Sheridan took him on.

And that's when he really started being a hero, was it?
Sorry. Not yet.

Why not? We're tired of waiting.
Louisa was having a baby – a daughter, Arta. So Bill went
home, looked round, then set off to make some quick money
for them.

How did he get it?
By killing buffaloes. The railroad was approaching and the men
who were building it needed feeding. So Bill killed at least 12
buffalo a day and the railway workers had their fill of buffalo
meat whether they liked it or not. They didn't. Well, tough (like
the meat). There was nothing else to eat.

But when he'd earned enough money, back he went to the Indian wars.

Did he become a hero now?
Yes, he did. General Sheridan was at Fort Hays. Buffalo Bill brought him news from Fort Larned which meant a big change of plan. New orders had to be got to Fort Dodge, 100 miles away. It could only be taken by horse, but nobody would go. Already many riders had been killed on the dangerous route.

Nobody?
Even before he had had a rest after bringing the news, Bill said, "I will."

And he did. He rode off to Dodge, got the news there in time, rode back to Fort Larned with more orders, then set off again for Fort Hays with the latest news for General Sheridan. And he got through, where many had died. Brave? Mad? Or what?

General Sheridan was so pleased that he made Bill chief scout for the 5th Cavalry with a colonel's pay. And this was enough to make Bill call himself 'Colonel' for the rest of his life.

Good. He's a hero at last. What came next?
Ah yes. The Battle of Wichita, against Chief Black Kettle and

the Cheyenne. A terrific victory for the US cavalry. Buffalo Bill and Wild Bill Hickok were in the thick of it. In fact, really, they won the battle on their own. Amazing. Whole books were written about their incredible heroism.

EXCEPT

It wasn't a battle. It was a massacre. The Indian camp was asleep and the army killed them all before they had time to wake up. Besides, Buffalo Bill and Wild Bill Hickok were hundreds of miles away at the time.

Still, that's how heroes are made.

Was Buffalo Bill never a hero at all, then?
Look, let's get this straight. He did some wonderful, brave things. But there were plenty of men in the Wild West who did as much. It's just that so many stories grew up about him saying he'd done even more than he had.

Why about Bill? Why not about some of the others?
For a very good reason, which is now just about to appear in the story.

NED BUNTLINE

Ah yes, I remember. The writer who wanted new stories for his novels about the Wild West.

That's the man. He knew people back east wanted to hear all about the stirring deeds on the frontier. He knew they wanted heroes they could admire, who did superhuman things. He also knew they weren't going to come out west to check on the facts.

Yes, Ned Buntline was looking for a hero. Here's the story about how he found one.

Ned thought he knew who he was looking for. Now we'll briefly hear about another character in the story, though Buffalo Bill didn't see him much – if ever at all.

CHIEF TALL BULL

Chief Tall Bull had united Sioux and Cheyenne in a force which was terrorising settlers. He had to be got rid of. With great bravery, Major Frank North stalked him over miles of hostile country. At last he found Tall Bull – and killed him.

Yes, Frank North was the man to be the next great Wild West hero.

Ned found him at Fort McPherson. But Frank didn't want to be made into a hero. "I know who could be, though," he said and pointed to someone asleep under a wagon. Ned crawled under to find out who it was and wake him up.

What did he see?

A tall young man rubbing the sleep out of his eyes.

An amazingly handsome, clean-cut face.

Brown eyes, brown hair to his shoulders and a little beard.

A reckless look in his eye, as if he didn't care about anything.

Broad shoulders and the look of an athlete.

It didn't matter that Bill was waking up with a hangover. Ned knew at once that he'd found the man he would make into America's greatest hero.

The first book that Ned wrote about Bill had him wiping out a whole gang of desperadoes, the McCandless Gang. Actually, Wild Bill Hickok did that. Then he wrote about Bill killing Tall Bull. As we have seen, that was Frank North. When they asked Frank whether he minded, he answered, "That's show business!"

★　　★　　★　　★

CHAPTER 5

Buffalo Bill Gets Famous

So now Buffalo Bill got rich, did he?

Of course he didn't. It's all very well having books written about you, but not so good if you aren't earning any money from them. He still had to scratch a living from somewhere.

What did he do?

One of the very first things didn't make him much money, but it had a huge effect on his life. People now believed that dinosaurs once roamed the Earth and scientists were looking for fossils. Some professors and students from Yale University wanted a guide to the badlands of the Bighorn Basin in Wyoming, a valley nobody went to because it was locked

between two mountain ranges. Bill took them. He wasn't much interested in fossils, but listened carefully to them talking, especially when a professor said that the Bighorn Basin might be dry and useless now but one day it would be fertile and prosperous.

Bill never forgot that, as we shall see.

But surely looking after professors wouldn't make him rich, would it?
No. What happened next did, though.

What was that, then?
Another character in Buffalo Bill's story entered. He was:

41

GORDON BENNETT

You mean that newspaperman?

That's him. As the Indians were driven further westwards, America was becoming safer. A lot of people back east wanted to see what it was like for themselves – especially rich people. So Gordon organised buffalo hunting parties for them. Who better as the guide than – BUFFALO BILL.

Yes, out they came in their special trains, all the high society of New York anxious to rough it for a little while. They were especially charmed to meet the legendary Buffalo Bill. Bill

loved it. He guided them all day and helped them shoot scores of buffalo. At night he held them spellbound with stirring tales of the West, some of them even true. He became a real star.

Did only Americans go on these expeditions?
Oh, no. First, out came the English dukes and earls. Then came the biggest catch of them all:

GRAND DUKE ALEXIS OF RUSSIA

Alexis thought Bill was great! But because he was a royal, he wouldn't be told what to do. He wouldn't use the rifle that was given him. He thought it was more sporting to shoot buffalo with his revolver. The trouble with that was the buffalo's hide is too thick for revolver bullets to get through. They just bounced off.

But if Alexis didn't shoot any buffaloes, war might be declared between Russia and the USA!

Bill got an Indian to hide behind a rock. As Alexis galloped by on his horse, screaming and firing his revolver wildly, the Indian calmly aimed an arrow at the buffalo and killed it at once.

And Alexis never knew! He killed eight more buffaloes that way! It was sorry and wasteful sport, and the Indians looked on aghast as their main food supply was left to rot.

But Gordon Bennett said, "Bill, you must come out east and meet the people who matter."

Who were they?
Millionaires, rich society women, writers like the great Mark Twain, all the people who were changing the United States into a country more like Europe than the Wild West.

Did he like it?
Not at first. He couldn't dance, he got drunk, he felt foolish in the fine clothes they bought him. He thought he'd be better

off back at home. Then he met Ned Buntline again. Once again, Ned did something very important.

What was that?
He took Bill to the theatre to watch a play. It was called *Buffalo Bill, King of the Border Men*. Here, Bill watched someone else trying to be him on the stage. Weird. And this actor was doing it very badly. Bill pretended he wasn't there. But then a theatre spotlight turned on him, everybody saw him and he had to make a speech. The theatre manager offered him a fortune if he would go on the stage and act himself.

"You may as well ask a mule to do it," Bill answered. To himself he said, "*I want to get out of here.*"

And did he?
Yes. Just in time. A message came from General Sheridan. Bill was needed as a scout again.

He was broke, he only had his society clothes and he spent his last few dollars getting drunk. He reported for duty in tailcoat and top hat, and nobody believed who he was.

But when he had convinced them, he led the cavalry into a battle against the Sioux in which nobody could deny he was

brave and clever – so brave that he won the Congressional Medal of Honour, which was one of the highest awards an American can receive.

Bill was very proud of this. There was one snag. It should only go to serving soldiers. And Bill wasn't one, because scouts weren't actually in the army. Just before he died, many years later, the Government took it away from him.

Let's hope he never found out.

★　　★　　★　　★

CHAPTER 6

"Oh, Mamma, I'm a Bad Actor"

I bet Bill never went near theatres again after that evening
with Ned.

Wrong. It's 1872 now and Buffalo Bill is 26 years old. If Ned
Buntline wanted to make money out of him, he couldn't hang
around. So he went to Chicago and set up as a theatre producer.
He would write the plays – and act in them – and Buffalo Bill
would play the lead as himself. He promised Bill a fortune.

Bill refused, of course.

No, he didn't. Louisa persuaded him. Besides, she needed to get
the money before he drank it all away. So off he went to Chicago,
to find nothing ready – no play, no actors. What a mess.

47

So he came home again.
No. Ned said it would be all right. He wrote a play, hired some actors and rehearsed it, with Bill in the lead, in one week.

Didn't you say that Bill had never acted in his life?
I did. So what happened? Did:

a) the play never open at all.

b) the play open on time but everybody hissed, booed, whistled and threw rotten eggs and tomatoes on the stage?

c) the whole cast get run out of town and the theatre smashed up?

All of them, probably, if it was that bad.
Well, you're wrong. *The Scouts of the Plain* was an awful play. The writing was dire, the acting was worse. But Ned was no fool. He knew two things:

a) if it was about the Wild West, people would flock to it. Lots of fights with Indians, thrilling rescues, triumph against all the odds – that's what they wanted to see.

b) if Buffalo Bill was on stage in person, they'd love it.

What was the play like?

I don't know. As far as I know, there's no copy still existing.

But the script might have looked something like this:

Scene: the valley of the Little Big Horn.
Enter Buffalo Bill and Ned Buntline.

Ned: Gee, Bill, we're sure in a fix now.
There's only us left to defend innocent
American womenfolk and their children.
We've got six rounds of ammunition left
between us and over the brow of the hill
there're 10,000 Sioux armed to the teeth
and ready to roll.

Bill: Aw, shucks, Ned, there ain't no cause
to fret. I reckon that with a dose of our
good ol' Yankee true grit we'll wipe those
danged Injuns off God's earth and make the
land safe for decent God-fearin' folk.

(Sounds off-stage of wild Indian
war-cries. Indians appear from wings in
feathered headdress and warpaint.)

Bill: Start shootin', Ned.

(Six shots sound. The six leading Indians
fall. Ned and Bill throw guns away)

Bill: I guess it's down to just our bare
hands now.

(Indians rush them. Ned and Bill knock
them out, trip them up and throttle them
one by one.)

49

.Ned (hurling Indian to ground): Another Indian bites the dust.

Bill (tripping another up): And another.

(Soon all Indians lie in heap on floor. Ned and Bill blow on their fists.)

Ned (coming to front of stage): Well, folks, that's another victory for America and it's all thanks to that steadfast hero of the Wild West, BUFFALO BILL.

(Audience wild with enthusiasm. Cheers and shouts of "Play it again, Bill." Curtain comes down. Indians get up.)

So, even though it was the worst play ever put on a stage, IT WAS A ROARING SUCCESS. It didn't even matter that Buffalo Bill, when he saw Louisa sitting in the audience, said that great line, "Oh, mamma, I'm a bad actor." The audience lapped it up.

What next?

After wowing Chicago, they toured around the United States: St Louis, Cincinatti, you name it, they were there. At last they came to New York. And now entered the next character in Buffalo Bill's story:

MAJOR JOHN BURKE, or ARIZONA JOHN

Was he the one who wasn't a Major and had never actually been to Arizona?

That's the one. And as soon as he entered, then goodbye, poor old Ned.

Why?

Ned was a rotten actor. Whenever he forgot his lines, he gave a speech against the evils of drink, which was a bit cheeky because he was never off the bottle himself.

Also he was a rotten manager. The play made a lot of money, but he arranged things so that he got most of it while Bill got hardly any. Which was wrong, because Bill need only stand on the stage and do nothing, and people would still flock from miles around to see him.

So they kicked Ned Buntline out. Arizona John became manager and the play was rewritten. But what about the part that Ned used to play?

Now Buffalo Bill had a brilliant idea – or so he thought. Did he:

a) say he'd do both parts himself?

b) give it to someone else in the cast?

c) get a proper, real and famous actor in to do it?

d) none of these, but something that, though it seemed a good idea at the time, in the end was a COMPLETE DISASTER?

From what I've picked up about Bill so far, it will be d). Dead right. The new addition to the company was to be – WILD BILL HICKOK.

Wild Bill only did it because he needed the money. He thought acting was for wimps. He hated stage lights. One night he got so fed up with being followed by a spotlight that he hid behind the scenery and shot it out with his six-shooter. Once he came on stage late, then forgot his lines. An actor, to cover up, said, "Why, Bill, what kept you so long?" Wild Bill then started

telling stories about his own deeds which weren't in the play and went on for hours because nobody dared stop him. When he finally shut up, the audience cheered him for hours. I have no idea what time the play finished that night. Nobody cared. Wild Bill's stories had been better than any daft old play.

Wild Bill lasted a year. One night he stood in the wings, watched the others act and said, "Ain't they foolish? I ain't gonna do it." Then he walked out.

And he and Buffalo Bill weren't friends any more. A pity. Three years later, someone shot Wild Bill Hickok in the back of the head while he was playing poker in a saloon. The Wild West was never the same again.

CHAPTER 7

Buffalo Bill in the Wars Again

Did Buffalo Bill spend the rest of his life with this awful play?
Far from it. In 1876, something happened which made plays
seem pretty stupid. His six-year-old son, Kit Carson Cody, died
of scarlet fever.

Yes, I know. No-one would die from such a thing nowadays.
But this was long before the days of vaccinations. Children
died from things nobody even gets nowadays – and if they do
it's curable.

There was only one thing for Bill to do now. No more plays –
he was off back to the wars with the Indians.

Weren't they over yet?

Far from it. In fact – THIS WAS THE BIG ONE. At the centre of it was another important person in Buffalo Bill's life:

CHIEF SITTING BULL

Was he the one we heard about earlier who united the tribes and beat General Custer?

Dead right.

Why did General Sheridan think Custer was a bit of a twerp?

First, because Custer believed the Indians would be a pushover.

Second, because he wouldn't work with the other generals. He wanted all the glory for himself. This made him reckless, especially with his soldiers' lives, which is the worst thing a general can be.

This is what happened:

Custer's orders were to wait for two other generals with their cavalry to meet him at the Little Big Horn. Then they would attack Chief Sitting Bull together. But Custer wouldn't wait. He thought Sitting Bull only had a few men with him.

Custer was wrong. He attacked Sitting Bull – and the whole of the 7th Cavalry were wiped out at the Battle of the Little Big Horn. It was the worst defeat the US Army had ever had.

Everyone was aching for revenge. Now Buffalo Bill came back into the wars to scout for the 5th Cavalry under General Merritt. They were sent on a march across the Black Hills of Dakota, to stop the Cheyenne from joining up with Sitting Bull's Sioux.

After marching for 80 miles, they found the Cheyenne. Now another character enters:

CHIEF YELLOW HAND

Picture the scene. On one side, the US 5th Cavalry. On the other side, the Cheyenne tribe. There's a famous painting depicting it. They should have been fighting. But they didn't. They just watched each other. And then –

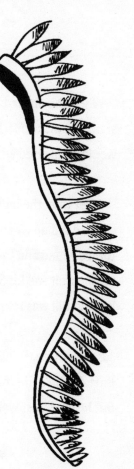

Chief Yellow Hand rode out and shouted his great challenge:

"*I know you, Pahaska.*"

Well, you know what happened next – Buffalo Bill's greatest triumph in the Indian wars. He won the duel and took Yellow Hand's scalp.

Ah, but you don't know what happened afterwards, do you?

Go on, tell us.
When Bill had taken Yellow Hand's scalp, he was so pleased with himself that he sent it back home to Louisa.

When she opened the parcel, the scalp was days old and stank the place out. Louisa was nearly sick. Bill thought she would be pleased with his little gift. Well, she wasn't.

After that, the Indian wars were soon over. The Cheyenne were so fed up when they saw their Chief killed that they turned round and the 5th Cavalry chased them back home. Sitting Bull and his Sioux ran for safety into Canada. Now Buffalo Bill was free to do what he liked again.

Just a minute. How could Sitting Bull be important in Buffalo Bill's life if he's out of the story already?
But he isn't. Just wait and see.

CHAPTER 8

Buffalo Bill the Great Showman

If Bill could do what he liked now, I bet he did something
extraordinary.

No, he didn't for once. He just went back touring with his
plays. But without Wild Bill to liven things up, it wasn't the
same. "There must be something better than this," Bill said to
himself. "If only..."

If only what?

Buffalo Bill had a GREAT IDEA. But it needed a lot of work to
make it happen.

What was it?

Be patient. While Bill was away scalping Yellow Hand, Arizona John Burke had the same GREAT IDEA.

Tell us, tell us!
All in good time. In 1882 they met a rival theatre producer who had exactly the same GREAT IDEA. He was another big character in Buffalo Bill's story and his name was:

NATE SALSBURY

Is that the one who was sentenced to death in the army?
That's the fellow. And THIS was the GREAT IDEA they all shared.

At last.
The Wild West wasn't won on a theatre stage. If people wanted to know what it was really like they would have to go outdoors. Why not take the shows outdoors for them?

Why not have – **BUFFALO BILL'S WILD WEST SHOW?**

Why not indeed? But think what organisation it would need, what brilliant publicity, what sheer hard work.

NEVER MIND. THESE THREE MADE A BRILLIANT TEAM:

Buffalo Bill – the big name, the real draw.

Arizona John – the advertising and publicity man.

Nate Salsbury – the design and the organization man.

Think of it. First, the posters go up in your town:

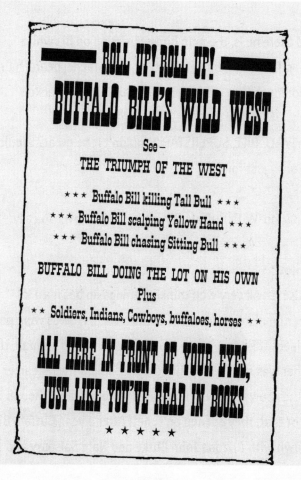

A herd of buffalo charging around the arena. Cowboys taming wild horses. Indian braves galloping and whooping round the Deadwood Stage as the coachman urges the horses on. You're deafened by gunfire. Smoke drifts across. The marksmen shoot glass balls thrown in the air and hit them every time. You see Buffalo Bill kill Tall Bull and scalp Yellow Hand *with your own eyes*, so the stories must be true.

And there he is, the man himself, sitting on his white charger. There's his handsome face, moustache, beard, hair to his shoulders. He's wearing his famous buckskin jacket.

BUFFALO BILL, SUPERSTAR. Wouldn't it be great? Wouldn't the money just roll in?

Sadly, no. With Buffalo Bill, things were never so easy.

Why not?

Because it's all very well thinking things up but it's a lot different making them work. To start with, crowds were poor, the places the show was put on in weren't good enough, the weather was rotten. They hired a Mississippi river steamer to take the show to New Orleans. But the boat sank (though in spite of that, they opened on time)! After a year, Buffalo Bill sat down with Arizona John Burke and Nate Salsbury and said,

"This sure ain't no good. We gotta think of something quick."

Don't worry, Buffalo Bill. Help is just round the corner.

★　　★　　★　　★

CHAPTER 9

Little Annie and the Big Chief

What was this help, then?

It came from two places. Bill thought of one of them himself. The other just turned up.

Here's the one which just turned up.

One day, Nate Salsbury was sitting in the office wondering what they could do to get things better when there was a knock at the door. He opened it – to find two people, a man and his wife.

"We're Mr and Mrs Frank Butler. We're a double act; we're

both crack shots," said the man. "Any chance of you giving us some work?"

Before Nate said, "Sorry, there's hardly any work for the people we've got already," he looked at them. The man seemed ordinary enough, but his wife – she was TINY.

He asked them to shoot. The man was pretty good, but his wife – she was FANTASTIC. She shot glass balls in the air, she shot as she rode a horse at full gallop, then she turned round in the saddle and shot just as well over her shoulder.

"I could use the wife in the show," Nate said to himself. "But I don't want *him*. He's not as good so we can't afford to pay him."

So what would Nate do? Would he:

a) tell the man to go away?

b) tell them both to go away?

c) take them both on and hang the expense?

He couldn't do a), he wouldn't do b) because another show might get her, so he had to do c).

Here's how he did it. Mrs Butler would do the shooting while Mr Butler would have a nice cushy job in the office.

Everybody was satisfied.

Except Nate. "We can't bill you as Mrs Butler," he said. "What was your name before you were married?"

"Annie Oakley," she answered.

So the legend was born and the next character in the story entered:

LITTLE ANNIE OAKLEY

So there you go. The Deadwood Stage and the buffaloes and the whooping Indians were all very well, but IT WAS LITTLE ANNIE EVERYONE CAME TO SEE.

And soon, someone else as well.

Who's that?
Who was the most famous Indian and the greatest warrior of them all, who could still shoot an arrow and wield a tomahawk?

Who led the Indians that won the battle of the Little Big Horn?

Who had the hatchet face that scared white folk to death?

Who spent his time in retirement writing poetry?

Well, we know really, except for the poetry, but just tell us again.

All right, it was – CHIEF SITTING BULL.

Buffalo Bill, Arizona John and Nate Salsbury all knew that if they were showing what the old Wild West was like, they had to get Sitting Bull on the show. But would he come? And would the audiences like him if he did? After all, he had killed General Custer and given Americans a nasty shock.

But they asked him. And he said he would.

What did he do in the show?
Nothing. Except sit on a horse in the middle of the arena while everything else swirled round him, and look FIERCE.

68

That's not much.

Given who he was, it was quite enough.

Why should he want to come at all, when Buffalo Bill was his enemy?

Because Bill and Sitting Bull respected and trusted each other. They were strong men who kept their word. Sitting Bull knew that the only white men he could trust were the ones he used to fight. It's often like that with old enemies.

And did the people like him?

Well, they booed him. And he just stared back at them. The louder they booed, the harder he stared. Sitting Bull didn't care. In fact, he was rather pleased.

So was Buffalo Bill. Because many people came to the show just to boo Chief Sitting Bull.

What could possibly go wrong now? Especially when Sitting Bull and Annie Oakley became such good friends.

Buffalo Bill's Wild West show was complete.

CHAPTER 10

Buffalo Bill Crosses the Ocean

Was everything all right now?

It surely was. The year was 1885. The Wild West show started touring America and everywhere it went, the crowds flocked in and paid their money. At last the city folk of the east were meeting the fabled heroes of the west.

I bet Buffalo Bill loved it.

Again, he surely did. He was 40 years old and had the whole country at his feet. All the great American cities – New York, Chicago, St Louis, Philadelphia, New Orleans – and most of the little ones came out in thousands to wonder at this amazing spectacle.

Here they are folks!

CHIEF SITTING BULL, LITTLE ANNIE OAKLEY

&

BUFFALO BILL

Bringing the Wild West to

YOU!!!

★ ★ ★ ★ ★

Think of it. Buffalo Bill's Wild West show is coming to your town. First, you hear a lonely engine whistle calling from far down the railroad. Then a long, long train comes winding in. The locomotive heaves and pants with steam and smoke as it pulls its 26 cars. Each car is painted white. On the sides in gold lettering is:

BUFFALO BILL'S WILD WEST SHOW

The train stops. Stagehands pour out, bringing the portable grandstand which they set up. Opposite, they erect a vast backcloth, painted with the mountains of Wyoming. When the animal pens are set up, the animals are let out: horses, buffaloes, mountain elk. Everything is done smartly and quickly, because Nate Salsbury knows how to organize men at work. The Deadwood stage is wheeled out. The arena swarms with Indians and cowboys. If you're lucky you might catch a glimpse of Little Annie, Sitting Bull, perhaps Buffalo Bill himself. But don't worry if you can't. Just wait for the first performance next day.

And then they pack up and go. All you ask is, "When are they coming again?"

Not for some time, I fear. Because Buffalo Bill is taking his show to foreign parts.

Where to?
Europe. First, Britain, then France, then Germany, then Italy.

What happened in Britain?
Everybody loved him. The crowds were as big as in America. Queen Victoria thought he was great. She saw the show twice. The Prince of Wales couldn't keep away. Lords and ladies thought being seen with Buffalo Bill was the best thing around that year. Bill was really sad when it was time to pack up and go to France.

But it was the same there, wasn't it?

Not at all. The French weren't interested in the Wild West,
Indians or the Deadwood stage. They watched the show in
silence and wondered what all the fuss was about. Until...

Until what?

Little Annie appeared. Oh, the French loved Little Annie. A tiny
woman who could shoot better than – well, nearly as well as –
the finest French soldiers was worth coming miles to see. So,
yes, in a different way after all, Bill's show was as big a hit in
France as anywhere else.

What happened in Germany?

Oh, they loved the show. But Buffalo Bill was worried.
Wherever they went, German army officers, with spiky hats
and monocles, followed them around, looking at the animal
pens, poking round the kitchens, making notes as the
stagehands unloaded.

Why? Did they think Buffalo Bill was a spy?
No. Thirty years later came the answer. In the First World War,
the huge German army moved quickly across Holland, Belgium
and France. Just like the Wild West show. Could they have
done it without those first lessons learned from Buffalo Bill?

Well, if Bill thought that, he might not have been too
pleased.

What about Italy?
They loved it, though the cowgirls were a bigger attraction
than the cowboys. But for Bill, the greatest moment was an
audience with the Pope. At least, that's what Bill called it. The
Pope, if anyone asked him, would say it was a quick blessing as
he was carried past on his chair.

There was one embarrassing moment. When the Indians saw the Swiss Guard in their weird stripy trousers, they wouldn't believe these were soldiers and laughed all the way through the Vatican. The Pope wasn't too pleased.

That was the end of the tour – and back to REAL TROUBLE.

★ ★ ★ ★

CHAPTER 11

Buffalo Bill and the Ghost Dancers

Trouble? What trouble?

The Wild West show had toured Europe without Sitting Bull. After a couple of years he'd had enough. But now it was easier to get big Indian chiefs to come in his place. Chief American Horse was the first and Chief Red Shirt came after him.

They came because they trusted Buffalo Bill, like they trusted many old soldiers who'd fought them. They understood each other. But they didn't trust the white men in charge now.

Why not?

The Indians had been given large parts of their lands back to live on in the way they always had. But now people in the government said this wasn't good enough and set up the Indian Bureau to make sure that what they wanted to happen, happened. Indians should farm their land, live in towns and raise animals instead of hunting them. Besides, all that land was needed for cattle ranching and new towns. So they pushed the Indians back into little pockets of the worst, most useless land there was. Then they set up the Indian Police to make sure they stayed there.

Guess who the policemen were.

I've no idea.
Other Indians. The Indians did not like it.

I don't blame them. What could they do about it?
Not a lot. Except – **DANCE THE GHOST DANCE.**

The what?
They believed that if they did this wild dance round a fire until they fell into a trance, a new leader would appear from the dead to drive the white man away and give them back their old lands.

The Indian Bureau was very worried about this.

Why? The Indian Bureau didn't believe it, surely?
Of course not. But it meant that there could be new Indian
wars. Something would have to be done.

What?
The best thing would be if Chief Sitting Bull said that the
Ghost Dance was wrong. Other Indians would listen.

A woman who supported the Indian cause tried to persuade
him. Unfortunately, he thought she wanted to marry him, so
that soon finished. What could be done now?

I know. They sent Buffalo Bill instead.
No, they didn't. Bill volunteered. But the Indian Bureau
wouldn't let him.

So what happened?

He went anyway. The army said he should, so he got ready, with nothing but a wagonload of Sitting Bull's favourite candy.

And he got there and Sitting Bull listened.

You should know Buffalo Bill by now. What do you think? Did he:

a) get a message to Sitting Bull saying he was on his way and everything would be all right?

b) journey unarmed and alone with amazing bravery through Indian country where the white man was hated?

c) get drunk?

Don't tell me. I'm afraid I know already.

Well, Bill wasn't into messages so he didn't do a). But someone else did, as we shall see. He DID do b). At least, he started off by doing b).

But he ended up doing c). On the way, Bill stopped for the night at an army camp, Fort Yates. There he started drinking with the officers. Next morning, he was still drinking but they were all asleep under the table. So he left them there and prepared to set off again.

What stopped him?

I said someone else sent a message. It was the Indian Bureau.
While he was drinking, they sent a telegram to Fort Yates
ordering Bill to stop. Instead, a force of Indian Police went, a
fight started and Sitting Bull was killed.

So Sitting Bull was killed by his own people.

What happened then?

The Indians rose up. The whole US army was ordered in. At
Wounded Knee they caught Chief Big Foot and 400 Sioux on
their way to join up with the others. The army had the first
ever machine guns. All the Sioux were killed.

There would be no more Indian wars.

Buffalo Bill was appalled.

Afterwards, he said that if he'd reached Sitting Bull first, the chief would still be alive and there would have been no Wounded Knee. Perhaps, but whose fault was it? The man who sent the telegram, the officers who got him drinking, or Bill for liking the whisky so much?

Still, it wasn't all gloom for Buffalo Bill. When the other Indians heard about Wounded Knee and surrendered, he found 100 of them for his show – including the Ghost Dancers. What a great act they would be!

CHAPTER 12

Away Again, Then Back With a Crash

If I were a Ghost Dancer, I wouldn't join up with Buffalo Bill.
Well, these did. What else could they do?

Did they like it?
Who knows? They never said. Now the Wild West show went abroad for three whole years, from 1891 to 1894. They went to Britain, where lords and ladies still flocked to see him; to France where they still loved Annie; to Germany where army officers still poked around seeing what went on; to Russia, where the Russians didn't like them very much, and all round Europe to places they hadn't been to before.

What the Ghost Dancers made of it all, I have no idea.

Then what?

They came back home. Buffalo Bill was nearly 50 now. His hair was pure white. His joints were creaking. He didn't do much more than Sitting Bull had years before – just sit in the arena on his horse and look round. All through America they went, just like before. But it wasn't the same.

Why not?

The Wild West show wasn't what it used to be. It was getting old, like Buffalo Bill. How long could it go on?

As long as he wanted it to, surely.

That's what he thought. Give it up while you're at the top, that's the best motto. Besides, he had other things going for him.

Such as?

Remember the professor who told him years before that the Bighorn Basin would one day be one of the most fertile parts of America? Bill never forgot. He bought land there. He built a dam and the Cody Canal, which gave the parched land water so it became rich and green. He set up a new town and called it CODY. Well, why not? He also set up a huge ranch, the T.E. Ranch, where Louisa lived and where he could retire to. One day.

Why not now?

Because he could never keep any money. He spent it all on whisky, gifts for his friends, both male and (sorry, Louisa!) female, setting up dodgy businesses which ended up being run by crooks who fleeced him.

So he had to go on with his Wild West show. On and on and on and on... And then...

One night in 1901, the train left Charlotte, Virginia, on its way to New York. How did the freight train coming the other way end up on the same track? There was a terrible head-on collision.

Amazingly, nobody was killed. But 100 horses died. And, worst of all...

Little Annie Oakley was badly injured.

She was paralyzed down one side, her hair turned white overnight and nobody thought she would ever shoot again. But she did, though it took her over a year to get better. But like so many in the show, she was never the same again.

Nate Salsbury was in a wheelchair. In 1902 he died.

Arizona John couldn't cope on his own. The show was sold to people who only wanted money out of it. They kept Bill on because he was still the big draw. But he didn't give the orders any more. He had to do what he was told.

Even the Indians were getting fat and slow.

Time to call it a day, I reckon, Bill.
I know. But he couldn't afford to.

On and on and on and on... until he had one last fling.

"LET'S MAKE PICTURES!" he said.

★   ★   ★   ★

CHAPTER 13

Buffalo Bill Goes into Films

What, like Arnold Schwarzenegger?
Not quite. The Wild West show was falling apart completely. In 1913 it went bankrupt. Everything was sold off – even Bill's favourite white horse, Isham.

That was a bit sad.
Don't worry. A friend bought Isham and sent him off to the T.E. Ranch, so he and Bill could retire together.

And did they?
Not yet. Buffalo Bill still had to go on working. But then he had his GREAT IDEA.

The first films were being made and shown all over the United States. Wild West films were the most popular. Bill thought they were awful – slung together in studios and no better than the plays he once acted with Ned Buntline.

Why not make films about real events, in the very places where they happened?

It sounds obvious now. But nobody thought of it before Buffalo Bill. He wanted to make films telling the whole story, with the real people playing themselves.

What next?

He borrowed money to make a film about the final showdown between the army and the Indians at Wounded Knee. He hired a cast of soldiers and Indians, and persuaded General Miles from the real battle to play himself.

Who directed it?

Bill did. He seems to have been rather good at it. General Miles was hard to please. He wanted 11,000 soldiers, like he had at the time. Bill only had 300, so he made them walk past the

camera 40 times. He never told the general that after the first time there was no film in the camera. He also had to stop the Indians from taking revenge and killing the general.

Was the film any good?
If you were to see it now, you wouldn't think so. It was silent, jerky and shot on one camera, like all the very early films.

How do you know? Have you seen it?
No, I haven't. Nor has anybody else unless they're over 90 years old. Unless they were copied in time, these old pictures have fallen to bits. The film they were shot on wasn't much good.

Was it a success?
Sort of. But in those days people would watch anything that moved on a screen. It didn't make Bill enough to be a great film producer. So he was just as broke as ever and had to go on touring with what was left of his once-great show.

Slowly and surely, it was killing him.

CHAPTER 14

The Death of Buffalo Bill

How long did he go on for?
As long as he could. In1916 the show came to Portsmouth,
Virginia. He stuck it out until the last performance was over.
Then he collapsed, worn out.

He wasn't even strong enough to be taken to the T.E. Ranch.
Instead, he was brought to his sister's house in Denver,
Colorado.

There, on January 10th, 1917, with his family around him,
he died.

Where was he buried?

Not back in Cody, Wyoming, as he wanted. There wasn't
enough money left. Instead, he was buried on Lookout
Mountain, Denver. He would not have liked that.

That's sad.

Ah, but he would have loved his own funeral. All his old mates
turned up, most of them with bottles of whisky in their
pockets. Instead of funeral coaches there were bright wagons
from the show. Six old girlfriends arrived and annoyed Louisa
very much.

They all had a great time and most people agreed that if the
old devil could look down and see it all, he'd have a good laugh
to himself and wish he could join in.

CHAPTER 15

So What's Left?

You tell me.

I'll try.

For a start:

He was a real hero (some of the time).

He was a great showman (most of the time).

He was someone nobody could forget (all of the time).

But what did other people think of him?

Louisa?

He's an untrustworthy rat (some of the time).

Wild Bill Hickok?

He was my great friend (until it all went sour).

General Sheridan?

The best scout I ever had (some of the time).

Ned Buntline?

A way of getting rich quick (until that went sour as well).

Chief Sitting Bull?

Once my enemy, then my friend. A pity he let me down in the end.

Chief Yellow Hand?

Always my enemy. But I want my hair back, please.

Arizona John?

A great partner.

Nate Salsbury?

Ditto.

Little Annie Oakley?

I made his show. But then, he made my name.

And so it could go on. While he was alive, everybody had their piece of Buffalo Bill. But they would all agree on one thing.

BUFFALO BILL WAS A GREAT MAN. Once seen, never forgotten.

Half – or more – of the stories which are told about him aren't true. But who cares? The truth about him makes him even more memorable.

If ever you're in the United States, try to get to the Yellowstone National Park. And when you've had your fill of that wonderful place, travel a little further on until you come to:

CODY, WYOMING

There you'll see the Buffalo Bill Museum, full of memories of his amazing life. You'll see the Buffalo Bill statue overlooking the town.

And through everything you'll feel the spirit of this man, still remembered, warts and all, while the little people round him are forgotten except as parts of his own story.